A Guide For Widows And Widowers

How to Get Your Affairs in Order

After The Death of Your Spouse

JULIE A. CALLIGARO

HOW TO USE THIS BOOK

This book will help you get your financial and legal affairs in order after the death of your Spouse. It's unfortunate that you have to confront these issues while you're grieving, but these problems and potential problems cannot be ignored or put on a back burner until you're feeling stronger.

You can solve these problems without my help, but following the suggestions in this book will streamline the process saving you time and conserving energy. Don't procrastinate, just take it one Chapter at a time and very soon you'll have your affairs in order and enjoy peace of mind.

The first eight Chapters discuss your financial affairs and the last seven Chapters your legal affairs. Read each Chapter, even the ones that don't seem to apply to you. Otherwise you may overlook something that is relevant and important.

This book does NOT include fill-in-the-blank Wills, Trusts, Powers of Attorney or Guardianship forms. If you want do-it-yourself legal documents this is not the book for you. In my 30 years as an estate planning and probate attorney, I've seen only regret and heartache from do-it-yourself legal forms.

However I have developed a set of forms and checklists that will help you organize your financial and legal information. They are free at www.wsbforms.com/widow/. See Page 7 for a list of the forms and checklists and instructions for downloading.

TABLE OF CONTENTS

TWO

APPLY FOR SOCIAL SECURITY AND OTHER BENEFITS

If you are entitled to Social Security or other similar benefits, you will not receive the money until you file a claim with the appropriate agency. The sooner you apply for the benefits, the sooner you will receive the money.

Social Security
The Social Security Administration is much more user friendly than it was when I wrote the first edition of this book. There are several ways to contact them:
- www.socialsecurity.gov
- 1-800-325-0778.

Apply for Survivor's Benefits
Apply as soon as possible by telephone or at any Social Security Office. But before you go to the Social Security office, call and make an appointment and ask what documents you must bring with you. You will need original documents or certified copies of the following but additional documents may be required so ask.
- Death certificate;
- Social Security numbers for you and your Spouse;
- Your birth certificate;
- Your marriage certificate;
- Dependent children's Social Security Numbers;
- W-2 forms or federal self-employment tax return for the most recent year;

- The name of your bank and your account number because your monthly benefit will be directly deposited into your bank account.

Lump Sum Death Payment
A lump sum death payment is a one-time payment of $255 and is paid in addition to monthly survivor's benefits. Apply for the lump sum payment at the same time you apply for other survivor's benefits from Social Security.

It is important to note that you may be entitled to the lump sum payment even if you are not entitled to survivor's benefits. **You must apply for the lump sum payment within 2 years of your Spouse's death.**

Railroad Benefits
If your Spouse worked for a railroad or for certain companies closely connected with the railroad industry, you will probably receive survivor's benefits from the Railroad Retirement Board rather than from the Social Security Administration.

Apply for survivor's benefits at the nearest Railroad Retirement Board office. There are Railroad Retirement Board offices in most major cities. Go to www.rrb.gov and click on the "Field Office Index" link at the bottom of the page to find the field office closest to you.

Veterans Benefits
If your Spouse was a veteran locate his or her military discharge papers and call the nearest Veterans Administration office or visit www.va.gov. Ask if you are entitled to benefits and, if so, apply.

Black Lung Benefits
If your Spouse was entitled to Black Lung benefits you may also be entitled to benefits. Call this toll free number for information 800 638 7072.

THREE

APPLY FOR INSURANCE BENEFITS

If you are entitled to insurance benefits, you will not receive the money until you file the necessary forms. And since most insurance companies don't pay interest, the sooner you apply for the benefits, the sooner you will receive the money and put it to work for you.

Life Insurance
There are two types of life insurance policies to consider:
1. Policies provided by your Spouse's employer.
2. Policies purchased by your Spouse.

Policy Provided by Spouse's Employer
Whether your Spouse was employed or retired at death, there may be coverage under a group life insurance policy provided by the employer.

Contact the department that administers employee benefits and ask if your Spouse is covered under a group life insurance policy, if you are the beneficiary and the procedure for applying for the benefits. Follow the procedure and apply for the benefits.

Policy or Policies Paid for by Spouse
Contact the agent and request a form to apply for the life insurance benefits. The insurance agent will send you the appropriate form and instructions for applying for the benefits. Follow the instructions and apply for the benefits.

If You Think There is a Policy but Can't Find it
If you have correspondence from an insurance company or canceled checks of payments made to an insurance company, there may be a life insurance policy in effect. Contact the company to determine if there is an active life insurance policy.

If You Are Not the Beneficiary

If you are not the beneficiary there is no point in applying for the benefits **unless**:
• your minor child (children) is the beneficiary; or,
• the primary beneficiary is deceased and there is no living secondary beneficiary; or
• your Spouse's estate is the beneficiary.

In any of these circumstances you will have to Probate your Spouse's estate before you can apply for the benefits. (See Chapter Seven)

Fraternal Organizations

Your Spouse may have purchased a life insurance policy from a fraternal organization, such as the Knights of Columbus. Regardless of who issued the policy, the procedure for applying for the benefits is the same:
a. locate the policy;
b. locate the insurance company;
c. determine who is the beneficiary;
d. if you are the beneficiary, determine the procedure for applying for benefits;
e. apply for the benefits.

Cancer Policies

A Cancer Policy pays a death benefit if the person whose life was insured dies of cancer. If your Spouse's death was caused by cancer and your Spouse's life was insured by a cancer policy, file a claim for benefits.
a. locate the policy;
b. locate the insurance company;
c. determine who is the beneficiary;
d. if you are the beneficiary, determine the procedure for applying for benefits;
e. apply for the benefits.

Credit Unions

Some loans from Credit Unions include death benefits or accidental death benefits. If your Spouse had a loan or loans from a Credit Union, contact the loan department and ask if the loan includes a death benefit. Be prepared with the loan number and your account number when you call.

Credit Cards

Some credit cards pay a death benefit at the death of the card holder. Contact the credit card company and ask if that company pays a death benefit at the death of the card holder. Be prepared with the credit card account number when you make the call.

Auto Insurance

If your Spouse's death was related to an automobile accident contact your auto insurance company and ask what benefits you are entitled to and how to apply.

List of Insurance Policies

Refer to the List of Life Insurance Policies discussed in Chapter One. Have you filed claims for all policies? If not, do so.

Revise the List as necessary to incorporate any changes since the death of your Spouse. For example, remove your Spouse's life insurance policies once you have cashed them in. Make certain your own policies are on the List.

FOUR

APPLY FOR RETIREMENT BENEFITS

If you are entitled to retirement benefits, the sooner you apply for them, the sooner you will receive the money. Call your Spouse's employer and ask for the department that administers survivor benefits. Explain that your Spouse was an employee (or retiree) and ask if you are entitled to survivor's benefits and, if so, how to apply for them.

Benefits You May Receive if Your Spouse Was Employed at Death

If your Spouse was employed at death, you may be entitled to a preretirement spousal benefit. If you are entitled to a preretirement spousal benefit:

a. the benefit will be a percentage of the retirement benefit your Spouse would have received had he or she lived to retire;

b. the benefit may not be paid to you until the date your Spouse would have reached retirement age;

c. the benefit will either be a monthly payment for the rest of your life or a one-time lump sum distribution.

If You Elect a Lump Sum Distribution

If you elect a lump sum distribution, depending on your age, you can choose either to take the lump sum immediately or roll it into your IRA (an IRA rollover.) Consult your accountant immediately. The decision you make will determine how much tax you pay and when you pay it.

If you elect to roll the lump sum into your IRA, request a "trustee to trustee transfer," which means the trustee of your Spouse's retirement plan transfers the lump sum directly to the trustee of your IRA. A trustee to trustee transfer avoids a 20% withholding tax on the amount of the distribution.

Your Spouse was Retired at Death

The type of benefit that you will receive, if any, will be determined by decisions your Spouse made prior to retirement. If your Spouse was receiving a monthly benefit, you may be entitled to a monthly benefit. However, the amount of the monthly benefit you will receive will almost certainly be less than the amount that your Spouse had been receiving.

Your Spouse's Employer Says You Are Not Entitled to Benefits

If your Spouse's employer tells you that you are not entitled to survivor benefits, and if you believe that information is incorrect, request a Summary Plan Description and a copy of the latest Participant Statement. Review the Summary Plan Description and Participants Statement.

If you still think that you are entitled to benefits, contact your attorney and ask if he or she is experienced in reviewing a Summary Plan Description and what the fee would be. If the attorney is experienced and the fee seems reasonable, schedule an appointment.

If your attorney is not experienced in reviewing a Summary Plan Description or if the fee seems unreasonable, look for another attorney. Your objective is to schedule an appointment with an attorney who is competent to review the plan description (for a reasonable fee) and tell you if you are entitled to benefits and how to collect them.

List of Pension Plans and Accounts

Refer to the List of Pension Plans discussed in Chapter One. Have you addressed all retirement plans and accounts? If not, do so.

Revise the List as necessary to incorporate any changes since the death of your Spouse. For example, a new IRA that you started to receive a rollover from your Spouse's pension plan.

FIVE

ORGANIZE AND MANAGE YOUR FINANCES

Your objective in Chapter 5 is to develop and implement a short-term financial plan that will see you through the first six months after your Spouse's death.

Maintaining your financial status-quo is sufficient unless your expenses exceed your income. If your expenses exceed your income, get help immediately. Consult a trusted, sensible and competent family member or friend. After six months, develop and implement a long-term financial plan.

Short-Term Plan:
• Determine your financial needs for the first six months,
• Develop a plan to meet those needs, and
• Implement the plan immediately.

Long-Term Plan:
• Project your **lifetime** financial needs,
• Develop a plan to meet those needs, and
• Implement the plan.

Determine Your Financial Needs for the First Six Months
To determine your financial needs calculate your monthly cash flow which is the amount of your monthly income minus the amount of your monthly expenses.

Calculate Your Monthly Cash Flow
Download the form titled Income and Expenses. In the Income section, list each source of income you receive and the amount of income that source contributes to your total **MONTHLY** income.

If you receive income from a source less often (or more often) than monthly, convert the income to its monthly equivalent and then enter it in the Income section.

For example, if you receive stock dividends of $300 every quarter, multiply $300 x 4 dividends. Your yearly dividend income is $1,200. Now divide the yearly dividend income of $1,200 by 12 months. Your "monthly" dividend income is $100. ($300x 4 = $1200 ÷ 12 = $100 per month).

Next, enter the amount of your monthly expenses in the "Expense" section. If you are billed for an expense less often (or more often) than monthly, convert the expenses to its monthly equivalent and then enter it in the Expense section.

For example, if you pay a property tax of $3,000 twice a year, multiply $3,000 by 2 payments. Your yearly property tax expense is $6,000. Now divide the yearly tax expense of $6,000 by 12 months. Your "monthly" tax expense is $500. ($3,000 x 2 = $6,000 ÷ 12 = $500 per month).

Funeral expenses are not included in the cash flow calculations because I assume you paid the funeral expenses shortly after the funeral. If the funeral expenses have not been paid, include it as an expense.

Develop a Short-Term Plan

There are only two possible short-term financial plans. If your monthly cash flow is a positive number implement the Positive Cash Flow Plan. If your monthly cash flow is a negative number, implement the Negative Cash Flow Plan. Choose the plan that fits your situation.

Positive Cash Flow Plan

If, after considering all of your expenses, your cash flow is a positive number, your short-term financial plan is to maintain the status quo. Be sure, however, that you have included all of your expenses in your calculation of cash flow. The Expenses section contains a list of the most commonly incurred expenses, but if you have expenses that are not included on the list, enter them in the section labeled "Other" and include them in your calculations.

Negative Cash Flow Plan

If your cash flow is a negative number, your short-term financial plan is to convert your negative cash flow to a positive. To convert to a positive cash flow **YOU MUST REDUCE YOUR EXPENSES TO AN AMOUNT THAT IS LESS THAN YOUR INCOME *AND* SET ASIDE SOMETHING FOR EMERGENCIES.**

Ruthlessly examine your expenses and eliminate all nonessentials. Simultaneously refrain from all purchases that are not **absolutely essential**. Treating yourself to something special is understandable but not possible. You must exercise restraint. If you don't reduce your expenses below the level of your income, you will quickly slide into financial crisis.

Summary of Negative Cash Flow Plan

1. Determine your income.
2. Determine your expenses.
3. Reduce your expenses to an amount that is less than your income and leaves something left over for emergencies.
4. Do not deviate from the plan.

Good Financial Habits and a Positive Credit History

It is important that you develop good financial habits and establish a positive credit history in your own name. To help you accomplish both of these objectives, pay all of your bills each month before the due date. If you were the "bill payer" before your Spouse's death, continue with the system that you have been using. If you were not the "bill payer," develop and follow a system that encourages you to pay your bills on time.

Action List

❏ Determine your monthly cash flow using the Income and Expense form.

❏ Develop a plan to achieve a positive monthly cash flow.

❏ Implement the plan.

❏ Pay all bills promptly.

SIX

TAXES

You have two objectives in Chapter 6: to determine if you need to consult a accountant now and to locate and organize the information you or your accountant will need to prepare your yearly tax returns.

Consult a Accountant Now if:
You should consult a accountant immediately if:
1. Your total assets exceed $5,250,000; or
2. You are receiving a distribution from your Spouse's retirement Plan; or
3. Your Spouse was self-employed; or
4. You and your Spouse paid quarterly tax payments.

Competent and timely tax advice is important in these circumstances because:
1. It may be possible to decrease or eliminate an estate tax by filing documents with your local probate court or by electing the "portability" provision.

2. If an estate tax is due, an estate tax return must be filed and the tax must be paid within nine months of your Spouse's death. The estate tax return is complicated and should be prepared by an accountant. If the estate tax is not paid within nine months you will owe substantial interest and penalties.

3. If you will receive a distribution from your Spouse's retirement plan you may have a choice between a monthly payment and a lump sum payment. It is important that you discuss these options with your accountant before selecting an option because there may be time limits that you must adhere to and there may be tax advantages or disadvantages depending on which type of payment you choose.

4. If your Spouse was self-employed, the business may have immediate tax liabilities that must be met.

5. If you and your Spouse paid quarterly tax estimates another payment may be due soon and the amount of the payment may change.

Yearly Tax Returns
Locate your last year's tax returns and insert them in a folder. As you receive 1099s from your employer and financial institutions insert them in the same folder. At the end of the year, you should have all the information in the folder that you will need to file your tax returns. As soon as you have all the necessary information either prepare the returns yourself or schedule a meeting with your accountant

Action List
❏ Consult a accountant immediately if:
- Your total assets exceed $5,250,000; or
- You are receiving a distribution from your Spouse's retirement Plan; or
- Your Spouse was self-employed; or
- You and your Spouse paid quarterly tax payments.

❏ Locate last year's tax returns and insert them in the folder.
❏ Add 1099s to the folder as you receive them.
❏ Prepare your yearly tax returns as soon as you have all the necessary information. Don't procrastinate.

SEVEN

PROBATE

Your objective in Chapter 7 is to determine if a probate of your Spouse's estate is necessary and, if so, to begin the process.

What is "Probate"?
Probate is a court procedure that transfers ownership of the assets of a deceased person to his or her heirs. It involves filing the Will (if one exists) with the Court, having the Will accepted by the Court, listing the assets, paying the debts, and distributing the remaining assets to the person(s) named in the Will.

If there is no Will, the procedure described above will be the same except the assets will be distributed according to the laws of the state in which the probate takes place.

Determine if You Have to Probate Your Spouse's Estate
To determine if a probate is necessary, you have to know whose name is on the title of your Spouse's the assets. Fortunately you already have this information if you completed Asset List described in Chapter 1.

Review the column entitled "How Asset is Titled." A probate will be necessary if:
1. ANY asset listed on the List is titled in your Spouse's name only; or
2. The beneficiary of your Spouse's life insurance policy or annuity is listed as the "Estate"; or
3. The primary beneficiary of your Spouse's life insurance policy or annuity is deceased and there is no secondary beneficiary named; or
4. Both the primary and secondary beneficiaries of your Spouse's life insurance policy or annuity are deceased.

It doesn't matter if your Spouse had a Will or didn't have a Will, a probate is necessary if any of the above situations exist.

Who will Receive the Assets if there is a Will?

If your Spouse left a Will, the assets will be transferred to the person(s) named in the Will. If you are that person, the assets will be transferred to your name.

What if You Are not Named in the Will?

In most states, as the surviving spouse, you will receive a portion of your Spouse's assets even if you are not named in the Will. Consult an experienced probate attorney.

Who Receives Your Spouse's Assets if there is no Will?

If your Spouse died without a will, the laws of your state will determine who will receive the assets. In most states, the surviving spouse receives a portion if not all of the assets. Consult an experienced probate attorney.

Do You Need an Attorney to Probate Your Spouse's Estate?

In most states it is possible to probate an estate without an attorney. But if you live in a large metropolitan area with a busy and crowded probate court or if you don't want the frustration and the responsibility of probate, retain an attorney to probate the estate for you.

If you decide to retain an attorney, retain an experienced probate attorney. Discuss fees and court costs with the attorney at your first meeting. If you are satisfied with the proposed fees, request that the attorney prepare a written" Fee Agreement" that confirms your verbal agreement. You and the attorney should sign two copies of the Fee Agreement with each of you retaining a signed copy.

When to Start the Probate?

It takes many months to probate an estate, so the sooner you start the sooner you will be done. Do not ignore the problem if a probate is necessary. If there are assets in your Spouse's name alone, you will not be able to transfer them to your name nor will you be able to sell them without a probate. Act now if you determine that a probate is necessary.

Will there be a Probate at Your Death?

If, at your death, there are assets titled in your name only, a probate will be necessary. In the near future consult an estate planning attorney (possibly the same attorney who probated your Spouse's estate) and develop an estate plan for the transfer of your assets at your death. See Chapter 11.

Action List

❏ Retrieve the Assets List described in Chapter 1.

❏ Review the "How Assets Are Titled" section.

❏ Are any assets in your Spouse's name only?

❏ Review the beneficiaries of all life insurance policies AND annuities and determine if:

• the primary beneficiary is deceased with no secondary beneficiary named.

• the primary and secondary beneficiaries are deceased.

• the primary beneficiary is your Spouse's estate.

❏ If a probate is necessary, consult an experienced probate attorney.

❏ Discuss fees and costs with the attorney and then commit your agreement to writing in a "Fee Agreement."

❏ Consult an estate planning attorney and develop an estate plan for you or revise your existing estate plan. See Chapter 11.

EIGHT

SPECIAL CIRCUMSTANCES

Did Your Spouse Own a Business?
Could There be a Lawsuit Because of Your Spouse's Death?
Problems Not Discussed in this Book.

Your objective in Chapter 8 is to decide if you face special circumstances and, if so, to decide what to do about them. Here are two circumstances to consider:
• Did your Spouse own a business?
• Could there be a lawsuit because of your Spouse's death?

If Your Spouse Owned a Business
If your Spouse owned a business consider the following:
1. The payment of your health insurance premiums.
Are your health insurance premiums paid by your Spouse's business? If so, make sure that the next premium payment and future premium payments are paid promptly so that there is no lapse in your health insurance coverage.

2. The payment of quarterly tax payments.
Did you and your Spouse pay quarterly tax payments rather than have taxes withheld from paychecks? If so, make sure that the next quarterly tax payment is paid on time and in the correct amount. You may need to consult your accountant.

3. The day-to-day management of the business.
Who is running the business? Is there a manager in place? Do you need to step in and manage the business?

4. The sale of the business.
If your Spouse was in business without a partner, should you sell the business? Seek the advice of a accountant, legal advisor, and a trusted and competent family member or friend. Do not make a hasty decision. If possible, wait at least six months before deciding what to do.

5. The sale of your Spouse's share of the business if he or she had a partner(s.)
If your Spouse was in business with a partner you probably won't have responsibility for day-to-day management. But you will have to decide what to do about your Spouse's share of the business.

If your Spouse and partner have a Buy-Sell Agreement, there's nothing for you decide as the sale of your Spouse's interest to the partner will be controlled by the Buy-Sell Agreement.

If your Spouse and partner did not have a Buy-Sell Agreement, you may choose to sell your Spouse's interest to the partner. Do not allow yourself to be pushed into a hasty decision. Consult with a accountant, legal advisor, and a trusted and competent family member or friend. If possible, wait at least six months before making a decision.

6. Pension plan.
If your Spouse funded his or her pension plan, contact the plan administrator and ask what your options are. You will find the name, address and phone number of the plan administrator on the pension plan statements. Consult your accountant before you take a distribution from the pension plan.

Could there be a Lawsuit?
If your Spouse's death was accidental, related to employment, or the result of improper medical treatment there may be the **possibility** of a lawsuit. Consult an attorney and ask him or her to evaluate whether or not a lawsuit is indicated. Ask the deadline (statute of limitations)

for filing the lawsuit and for a referral to the type of attorney who specializes in your type of case. If a lawsuit is indicated, it must be filed with the proper court within the deadline or you will lose your opportunity to file the lawsuit.

How to Solve Problems Not Discussed in this Book
You may have a situation or problem not discussed in the preceding chapters.

If so, do not ignore it or consider it unimportant just because it's not covered in the book. Instead, apply the same procedure you have used to resolve your other legal and financial problems:

1. Identify the problem.
2. Consult resources and advisors as necessary.
3. Develop a plan for solving the problem.
4. Implement the plan.
5. Do not procrastinate or delay. Delay may be costly and there is satisfaction and pleasure in exercising control over your life again.

Action Plan
If Your Spouse Owned a Business:
❏ Does the business pay your health insurance premiums? If so, make sure the premiums are paid on time.

❏ Are quarterly tax payments due? If so make sure they are paid on time and in the correct amount.

❏ Who is managing the business?

❏ Postpone for 6 to 9 months, if possible, decisions about the sale of the business.

❏ Is there a Buy-Sell Agreement?

❏ Seek advice regarding the value of the business before you agree to sell.

❏ Apply for survivor's benefits from your Spouse's pension plan.

A Lawsuit?
❏ If appropriate consult an attorney.

❏ Diary the deadline for filing a lawsuit and make certain it's filed on time.

Problems Not Discussed

❑ Are there important situations or problems that you have overlooked? If so,
• Identify the problem.
• Consult resources and advisors as necessary.
• Develop a plan for resolving the issue or solving the problem.
• Implement the plan.
• Do not procrastinate or delay.

CONGRATULATIONS!

Your Finances Are Organized and in Order

Recap:
1. You have an up-to-date List of Assets and Debts in a format that will be easy to keep current.
2. You have applied for Social Security and/or the other benefits to which you are entitled.
3. You have filed life insurance claims for all policies that name you as the beneficiary.
4. If appropriate, you have applied for survivor benefits from your Spouse's employer.
5. If appropriate, you have elected either a lump sum or IRA roller after consulting with your accountant.
6. You are following a 6 month Financial Plan.
7. You have consulted your accountant if your combined assets (including life insurance on your life and your own retirement/pension accounts) exceed $5,250,000 and/or your Spouse owned a business.
8. You have determined if you need to start a Probate.
9. You have consulted an attorney if your Spouse's death could result in a lawsuit.

Your next step is to review your current estate plan if you have one and revise it if necessary. If you do not have an estate plan, it's time to do it. Your estate plan will have two objectives:
1. Appoint people you trust to manage your finances if you become incapacitated and to make medical decisions for you if you cannot make them for yourself.
2. Develop a plan to transfer your assets at your death to the person(s) you want to receive them.

Chapters Nine through Fifteen will help you meet these objectives.

NINE

WHO SHOULD PREPARE YOUR ESTATE PLAN?

I recommend that you hire an *experienced* estate planning or elder law attorney to prepare the legal documents that will make up your estate plan. If you had to Probate your Spouse's estate, that attorney may be a good choice.

I also recommend that YOU control your estate plan. You tell your attorney what you want your plan to accomplish. Ask your attorney what options you have including the cost and the pros and cons of each option. Then you decide (not your attorney) which options best meet your objectives.

How to Locate an Attorney
You want an estate planning or elder law attorney - an attorney who does estate planning for a living and not as a sideline. Your best source of information is a satisfied customer, so ask family and friends for suggestions. Your accountant and financial planner are also good sources of recommendations. Another source is your local Bar Association; call and ask for the names of estate planning and elder law attorneys in your area.

Cost of the Initial Consultation
Most estate planning and elder law attorneys do not charge for an initial consultation. Take advantage of a no cost consultation because it will give you the opportunity to judge whether you feel comfortable with the attorney and what his or her fee will be for the documents you want prepared.

I'm sorry to say that some attorneys do not treat their clients well. If you are not treated respectfully by the attorney and staff; if you are kept waiting for an unreasonable amount of time; if fees are not readily and thoroughly explained; if your estate plan cannot be done in a timely manner or if your phone calls are not returned promptly, find another attorney. There are a lot of us out there.

Questions to Ask the Attorney

1. Is estate planning your primary area of practice?

2. How do you charge, flat fee or hourly?

3. If the charge is hourly, what is your best estimate of the total fee?

4. If I have questions will I be able to contact you personally by phone or email?

5. Do you return calls or emails promptly?

6. If you will be drafting a revocable living trust, will you also prepare the documents that will transfer my assets to the trust? Is that included in the fee for the trust or is there an additional cost? **If the attorney will not prepare the documents that transfer your assets to your trust, find another attorney!**

7. How long will the process take from start to finish? If you are about to take a trip and want your estate plan in place before you leave, be sure you tell the attorney at your first meeting.

Before You Meet with an Attorney

Go to www.wsbforms.com/widow and download and fill in the forms in the "Take to the Meeting with an Estate Planning Attorney" section. Fill in the blanks and take them to your first meeting with the attorney. Also take your List of Assets and Debts and your Lists of Insurance Policies and Retirement Plans.

Action Steps

❑Ask family, friends or co-workers for the name of an estate planning or elder law attorney.

❑Schedule an appointment with the attorney and confirm that the initial consultation is free.

❑Before you meet with the attorney go to www.wsbforms.com/widow and download the forms in the "Take to the Meeting with an Estate Planning Attorney" section. Fill in the blanks and take the forms to the meeting. Also take your List of Assets and Debts and Lists of Insurance Policies and Retirement Plans.

❑Meet with the attorney and discuss your objectives and your options.

❑If you like the attorney, feel satisfied that you understand your options and that the fee is fair, engage the attorney to prepare the documents needed to create your estate plan.

❑Put the documents in a safe place. Tell your family where to find the documents and make certain they can access them.

TEN

POWERS OF ATTORNEY

Who Will Manage Your Finances if You Become Incapacitated?
You can appoint a child, family member of friend to manage your finances if you become incapacitated with either a financial power of attorney or a living trust.

Financial Power of Attorney
A financial power of attorney is a legal document that appoints someone you TRUST as your "agent" should you become incapacitated. You may need this person to pay your bills, do your banking, file your tax returns, collect rents, etc. A power of attorney takes effect either at the time you sign the document <u>or</u> at the time you become incompetent. Be sure to discuss these options with your attorney.

Four Important Points About Financial Powers of Attorney:
1. You cannot sign a Power of Attorney if you are incompetent, so advance planning is essential.

2. A Power of Attorney gives your agent the power and authority over your finances, so choose a person you **trust.**

3. Name an alternate in case the first person you name is not available or able to act as your agent.

4. A Power of Attorney terminates at your death.

Living Trust (which is discussed in detail in the next Chapter)
A living trust is an alternative to a financial power of attorney because if you have a trust and then become disabled or incompetent, your successor trustee is authorized to take over the management of the trust assets during your disability or incompetence.

Who Will Make Medical Decisions for You if You Cannot Make Them for Yourself?

Medical Power of Attorney

A medical power of attorney is a legal document that appoints someone you TRUST to make medical decisions for you if you cannot make decisions yourself. You can appoint your child, family member or friend. A medical power of attorney is also known as health care proxy and patient advocate designation.

Four Important Points About Medical Powers of Attorney:

1. You cannot sign a Power of Attorney if you are incompetent, so advance planning is essential.

2. A Power of Attorney gives your agent the power and authority to make your medical decisions, so choose a person you **trust.**

3. Name an alternate in case the first person you name is not available or able to act as your agent.

4. A Power of Attorney terminates at your death.

Living Will

A living will is a document that expresses your wishes concerning the use of artificial or life-support measures if there is no reasonable expectation you will recover.

I strongly recommend that you have a face to face discussion about end of life decisions with the people you appoint to make medical decisions for you. If your children have to make a "turn off the machine" decision, it will be easier for them if you've discussed with them how you feel and what you want and expect them to do.

Estate Plan

Financial and Medical Powers of Attorney are two of the documents included in an "Estate Plan." The other Estate Plan documents are discussed in the next Chapters.

Action Plan

❑Your attorney will prepare the necessary documents that will appoint someone you trust either by a Power of Attorney or by a Living Trust to manage your finances if you become incapacitated or incompetent.

❑Your attorney will prepare the necessary documents that will appoint someone you trust to make medical decisions for you if you cannot make the decisions for yourself.

❑Have a face to face conversation with the people you've named to make medical decisions for you.

ELEVEN

TRANSFER YOUR ASSETS AT YOUR DEATH

This Chapter is an overview of the different ways you can transfer assets at your death. Chapters 12, 13 and 14 discuss estate plans if you have minor children, adult children or no children

There are Five Ways to Transfer Assets at Death:
1. Beneficiary Designation;
2. Joint Ownership;
3. Will;
4. No Will;
5. Living Trust.

Some combination of these documents, together with Financial and Medical Powers of Attorney, constitute a typical "Estate Plan."

1. Beneficiary Designation
Certain types of assets allow you to name a beneficiary who will receive the asset at your death. Assets that pass by beneficiary designation go directly to the beneficiary thereby avoiding Probate.
However, if your beneficiary dies before you and you have not named a secondary (also called contingent) beneficiary the asset must be probated.

Examples of assets that allow you to name a beneficiary are: life insurance policies, annuities, IRAs, and certain types of bank and brokerage accounts. Bank and brokerage accounts that allow you to name a beneficiary or beneficiaries are called "Transfer on Death" (TOD) or "Pay on Death" (POD).

2. Joint Ownership

If an asset is titled in your name and the name of another person as "joint tenants with rights of survivorship," the asset passes directly to the joint tenant(s) at your death thereby avoiding Probate. Examples are deeds, bank and brokerage accounts, savings bonds and stock certificates.

If, however, your joint tenant dies before you die, the asset will then be in your name alone. And unless you add a new joint tenant, the asset must be probated at your death.

There are risks and disadvantages in holding an asset as a joint tenant with someone other than a spouse. They are:

1. To sell the asset you must have your joint tenant's cooperation and participation. For example, if you are selling your house and your son is a joint tenant, he and his wife must also "sign off" before you will be able to complete the sale.

2. The asset is vulnerable to your joint tenant's divorce, lawsuits and creditors. For example, if your daughter is a joint tenant on your bank account and she is sued, her creditors can collect from your bank account.

3. Will

If your assets pass to your children, family member or friend by Will, THE ASSETS MUST GO THROUGH PROBATE. The preceding sentence may surprise you as most people believe that if they have a Will, they have avoided Probate. Not true. If assets pass by Will, they must go through Probate.

Why so? A Probate is required to transfer title of the assets from the deceased person's name to the person(s) name in the Will.

A Will also names the person who is to administer your estate (the personal representative or executor) and who is to be guardians of minor children.

4. No Will

If, at your death, there are assets in your name alone and you do not have a Will, your assets must be probated and the laws of the state in which you live will dictate who will receive them.

5. Living Trust

A Living Trust is similar to a Will because it names who is to receive your assets at your death and who is to administer the Trust (the trustee).

You create a Living Trust by signing a legal document called a Trust Agreement. You are the trust maker, the trustee and the beneficiary. You can change or revoke your trust at any time.

As the trustee and beneficiary, you manage and have full use of the trust assets during your lifetime. If you become incompetent and at your death, the person you have named as your successor trustee takes over.

A living trust is especially useful if your become disabled or incapacitated because your successor trustee is authorized to take over the management of the trust assets. If a successor trustee does take over because of your illness or incapacity, the trust assets are used *exclusively* for your support and care.

A Trust CAN Avoid Probate

At your death your successor trustee distributes the trust assets to the person or persons you've named as the beneficiaries of your trust. If your assets are in the name of your Trust, the assets will pass directly to the trust beneficiaries avoiding Probate. However, if your assets are not in the name of your Trust, the assets must first go through Probate to get to your trust beneficiaries.

Your attorney will transfer your assets to your trust by changing the title of each asset from your name into the name of your trust. If you have a trust but your assets have not been transferred into the trust, contact your attorney immediately.

The primary difference between a will and a trust is a trust can avoid probate. A will cannot avoid probate.

Other Reasons to Use a Living Trust

Trusts are used for reasons other than avoiding probate. Trusts are also used to safeguard distributions to minor children and to protect governmental benefits that are or may be received by disabled children and/or adults.

Avoiding Probate

You will avoid Probate if:

1. Your assets pass by beneficiary designation and the beneficiary survives you.

2. You hold title as joint tenant with right of survivorship and the joint tenant survives you.

3. You have a living trust and your assets are in the name of your trust.

Action Steps

❏ Your objective is to set up an estate plan that transfers your assets at your death.

❏ Your action plan is to consider the options presented in this Chapter so you are prepared to meet with an estate planning attorney.

❏ Your attorney will prepare the necessary documents that will transfer your assets at your death.

❏ How to find an attorney, what questions to ask and what information to take to the first meeting was discussed in Chapter Nine.

TWELVE

ESTATE PLANNING IF YOU HAVE MINOR CHILDREN

Estate Plan if You Have Minor Children

Your attorney will prepare documents that accomplish the following:

1. Name a guardian or guardians for your minor children.
2. Implement a Trust or Will that protects your children's inheritance.
3. Name a trusted person to manage the children's money.
4. Name a trusted person to make medical decisions for you if you are unable to make decisions for yourself.
5. Name a trusted person to manage your finances if you become disabled.

The Difference Between a Guardian and a Trustee
A guardian is responsible for the child. A trustee is responsible for the child's money.

How to Name a Guardian
You name a guardian or guardians for your children in a Will.

Who to Choose as Guardian
The following information will help you select a guardian for your minor children. It's prudent to talk to the person(s) you have in mind to be sure they are willing to act as your children's guardian before your attorney prepares the documents.

Most parents strive to name a guardian who shares their values. Elements to consider include the proposed guardian's religious background, lifestyle and living situation.

Since the financial responsibility will rest with a trustee, the guardian's financial qualifications are of lesser importance. Nevertheless your child will certainly be influenced by the guardian's behaviour so choosing a person who is financially responsible is important. If the person named as guardian is also qualified to manage the child's or children's money, the guardian can also be the trustee.

Although nothing prohibits you from appointing someone who resides in another state, take residency into consideration especially if the proposed guardian lives far away from other family members.

Individual vs. a Couple
Parents often name a married couple to be guardians. Consider, however, who would remain the guardian in the event the couple divorces or one member of the couple dies. Often when pressed on this issue, "my sister and brother-in-law" is really "my sister." In the event of your sister's death, do you want your brother-in-law or someone else to be the guardian? Your Will should reflect your true preference by naming only the desired individual or individuals. Nevertheless if a couple is appropriate name them.

A Sibling
You can name an adult child to act as the guardian for your younger children. Although this may help maintain family stability, it's a substantial responsibility for the older child. In addition to the enormous change moving from the role of older sibling to the role of stand-in parent, the responsibility associated with acting as guardian may put too much pressure on the siblings' relationship. In seeking the best solution for the younger children, this plan has the potential to cause unintended harm to your older child.

How to Protect Your Children's Inheritance

1. Living Trust

As previously discussed, a Living Trust names who is to receive your assets at your death and who is to administer the trust (the trustee).

As the trustee and beneficiary, you manage and have full use of the trust assets during your lifetime. If you become incompetent and at your death, the person you've named as your successor trustee takes over.

Your attorney will transfer your assets to your trust by changing the title of each asset from your name into the name of your trust.

At your death, your successor trustee will use the trust assets for your children following the guidelines that you have specified in the trust. For example, you may direct your trustee to use the trust assets for your children's support, health, education and welfare. Your guidelines may be quite general or very specific.

The trust will also tell the trustee when to distribute the trust assets that have not been used for the child's health, education etc. You can direct the trustee to make a lump sum payment at the age you specify. Or you can direct the trustee to make two or more installment payments. Most parents choose to keep their children's inheritance in trust until their children are 21-30 years or older and distribute the inheritance in two or three installments.

Children with Special Needs

If you have a child with "special needs" who receives or may receive government benefits, an inheritance may make the child ineligible for the benefits. A Living Trust with *specific special needs provisions* will safeguard the child's benefits.

Selecting a Trustee

The trustee will be the person responsible for managing and distributing your child's inheritance. Therefore, he or she should have successful financial and investment experience <u>and</u> share your views about money.

The guardian and trustee may be the same person but they don't have to be. The decision is yours. If the guardian and trustee are not the same person, keep in mind that they will have to peacefully co-exist for the benefit of your children for what could be a long time.

Age is also a factor. While the children's grandparents may be the best choice today, as they get older, they may no longer be the best choice.

If your trust will continue after your children turn 18, the guardian will be out of the picture but the trustee will continue until your youngest child reaches the latest age you specified in the Trust.

Always, Always Name Backup Guardians and Trustees

For all the reasons I've discussed above, I emphasize naming backups for both the guardian and trustee. Better still, review and revise (if necessary) your estate plan regularly. If you've named grandparents as guardian and/or trustee and that's no longer in your children's best interests, revise your estate plan documents. Revisions are usually not expensive because you are amending your existing documents rather than starting from scratch.

Other Reasons for Using a Living Trust

Trusts are used for reasons other than protecting the finances of minor children. Trusts are also used to safeguard governmental benefits that are or may be received by disabled children. And trusts, if properly funded, avoid probate.

2. A Testamentary Trust

A Will that creates a trust at your death (a Testamentary Trust) is an economical alternative to a Living Trust. A Testamentary Trust will accomplish most of the same objectives as a Living Trust. A Living Trust goes into effect while you're alive. A Testamentary Trust goes into effect at your death.

Summary of Your Estate Plan

Your estate plan must include a Will because that's how you name guardians for your children. You will also need either a Living Trust or to include a Testamentary Trust in your Will. Either option will protect your children's finances. You may, however, have other important objectives that can only be satisfied by a Living Trust. Discuss these options in detail with your attorney.

Final Steps in the Estate Planning Process

Once you have an estate plan in place there are four more steps to take:

1. Place your original will, trust, etc. in a safe place.
2. Inform the person(s) you've named as guardian and trustee, power of attorney, executor or personal representative where they will find the documents at your death.
3. Make sure that person can access the documents. For example, if you keep these documents in a safe deposit box, will they be able to gain access to the box? If the name and signature of the person who will be managing your affairs is not on the bank's signature card, they won't have access to your documents at your death.
4. Attach an up-to-date List of Assets and Debts to your Will or Trust.

Action Steps

❏ Ask family, friends or co-workers for the name of an estate planning attorney.

❏ Schedule an appointment with the attorney and confirm that the initial consultation is free.

❏ Before you meet with the attorney ask your intended guardian and trustee if they are willing.

❏ Go to www.wsbforms.com/widow and download the forms in the "Take to the Meeting with an Estate Planning Attorney" section. Fill in the blanks and take them to the meeting with the attorney. Also take your List of Assets and Debts and Lists of Insurance Policies and Retirement Plans to the meeting.

❏Meet with the attorney and discuss your objectives and your options to meet those objectives.

❏If you like the attorney, feel satisfied that you understand your options and the fee is fair, engage the attorney to prepare the documents needed to meet your objectives and create your estate plan.

❏Put the documents in a safe place. Tell your family where to find the documents and make certain they can access them.

A Parental Consent Form for Minor Children and a Medical Information Form for Minor Children are available at www.wsbforms.com/widow.

THIRTEEN

ESTATE PLANNING IF YOU HAVE ADULT CHILDREN

An Estate Plan if You Have Adult Children

Your attorney will prepare documents that accomplish the following:
1. Name a trusted person to make medical decisions for you if you are unable to make decisions for yourself;
2. Name a trusted person to manage your finances if you become disabled;
3. Transfer your assets to your children at your death. You have five options:

- Beneficiary Designation;
- Joint Ownership;
-Will;
-No Will;
-Living Trust.

Depending on your circumstances, needs and desires, there are advantages and disadvantages to each of these options. For example, if you have one or two children and the appropriate types of assets, using beneficiary designations and joint ownership may be an economical and effective method of transferring your assets to your children at your death.

On the other hand, if a child has predeceased you, you may (or may not) want your deceased child's share to go to his or her children (your grandchildren). In that case a living trust is the most effective method of transferring your assets.

If you have an adult child with special needs, a living trust with very specific provisions will safeguard any governmental benefits your child receives or may receive in the future.

It may be extremely important to you that your avoid probate for your children. If so, you want to transfer your assets to your children by living trust and not by will.

As you can see, estate planning is **NOT** one size fits all. That's why I urge you to retain an *experienced* estate planning attorney to prepare your documents.

Final Steps in the Estate Planning Process

Once you have an estate plan in place there are four more steps to take:

1. Place your original will, trust, powers of attorney, etc. in a safe place.

2. Inform the person(s) you've named as trustee, power of attorney, executor or personal representative where they will find the documents at your death or disability.

3. Make sure that person can access the documents. For example, if you keep these documents in a safe deposit box, will they be able to gain access to the box? If the name and signature of the person who will be managing your affairs is not on the bank's signature card, at your death they won't have access to your documents.

4. Attach an up-to-date List of Assets and Debts to your Will or Trust.

Action Steps

❑Ask family, friends or co-workers for the name of an estate planning or elder law attorney.

❑Schedule an appointment with the attorney and confirm that the initial consultation is free.

❑Before you meet with the attorney go to www.wsbforms.com/widow and download the forms in the "Take to the Meeting with an Estate Planning Attorney" section. Fill in the blanks and take them to your first meeting with the estate planning attorney. Also take your List of Assets and Debts and Lists of Insurance Policies and Retirement Plans to the meeting.

❑Meet with the attorney and discuss your objectives and your options.

❑If you like the attorney, feel satisfied that you understand your options and the fee is fair, engage the attorney to prepare the documents needed to create your estate plan.

❑Put the documents in a safe place. Tell your family where to find the documents and make certain they can access them.

FOURTEEN

ESTATE PLANNING IF YOU DON'T HAVE CHILDREN

Estate Planning for You is <u>Critical!</u>

Why is it critical? If you die without an estate plan in place, your assets will go your closest living relatives. Who are your closest living relatives? Usually (each state has its own laws that answer this question) it's a parent or parents if they survive you. If not, grandparents if they survive you. If not, it's siblings if they survive you. If none of your siblings survive you it will be the children of your deceased siblings, your nieces and nephews.

That means everything you've worked for and saved could go to someone you haven't seen in years and maybe don't even know. It's foolish to put this off.

What is an Estate Plan if You Don't Have Children?

Your attorney will prepare the documents that accomplish the following:

1. Name a trusted person to make medical decisions for you if you are unable to make decisions for yourself;
2. Name a trusted person to manage your finances if you become disabled;
3. Transfer your assets to the individuals of your choice at your death. You have four options:

-Beneficiary Designation;
- Joint Ownership;
-Will;
-Living Trust.

Final Steps in the Estate Planning Process

Once you have an estate plan in place there are four more steps to take:

1. Place your original will, trust, powers of attorney, etc. in a safe place.

2. Inform the person(s) you've named as trustee, power of attorney, executor or personal representative where they will find the documents at your death or disability.

3. Make sure that person can access the documents. For example, if you keep these documents in a safe deposit box, will they be able to gain access to the box? If the name and signature of the person who will be managing your affairs is not on the bank's signature card, at your death they won't have access to your documents.

4. Attach an up-to-date List of Assets and Debts to your Will or Trust.

Action Steps

❑ Ask family, friends or co-workers for the name of an estate planning or elder law attorney.

❑ Schedule an appointment with the attorney and confirm that the initial consultation is free.

❑ Before you meet with the attorney go to www.wsbforms.com/widow and download the forms in the "Take to the Meeting with an Estate Planning Attorney" section. Fill in the blanks and take them to your first meeting with the attorney. Also take your List of Assets and Debts and Lists of Insurance Policies and Retirement Plans to the meeting.

❑ Meet with the attorney and discuss your objectives and your options.

❑ If you like the attorney, feel satisfied that you understand your options and the fee is fair, engage the attorney to prepare the documents needed to create your estate plan.

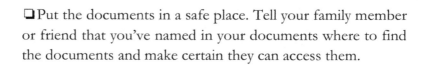❑Put the documents in a safe place. Tell your family member or friend that you've named in your documents where to find the documents and make certain they can access them.

FIFTEEN

KEEP YOUR AFFAIRS IN ORDER

Keep Your Affairs in Order
Now that your financial and legal affairs are in order, keep them up-to-date.

Schedule periodic reviews of:
Assets and debts,
Insurance policies,
Pension\retirement plans,
Estate plan,
Tax matters.

Review these issues yearly and at all family events that change your circumstances, i.e. remarriage, births, death, divorce, employment changes, retirement and the purchase or sale of significant assets.

Schedule Reviews
Incorporate periodic reviews of your financial and legal affairs into your day planner or diary system. But reminding yourself to review a specific financial or legal matter is useless if you don't actually review it and make any necessary changes.

The Location of Your Documents and Other Important Information
Your objectives are to:
1. Provide information to your family about your doctors, other health personnel and your medications.
2. Provide information to your family about the people to contact in an emergency.
3. Provide information to your family about your financial and legal advisors.

4. Provide information to your family about a prearranged funeral and\or burial.

Go to www.wsbforms.com/widow/ and download the Location of Important Documents form. Fill in the information and then place the list in a secure but accessible place. Tell your family where to find the information and make certain they can gain access. For example, if you place the list in your safe deposit box, be sure your children or family member know where the box is, where to find the key and are named on the bank's signature card.

Records Stored in Your Computer
If some of your records are stored in your computer:
Make a backup of these records and put the backup in a safe place; *a place that you will remember.*

Prepare a set of instructions for your family so they will be able to access this information. A detailed computer file of important information is useless if your family doesn't know it exists or knows it exists but can't find it or access it.

Prepare a list of your user name and passwords for on-line banking, email, frequent flier accounts, etc.

Action Plan
❑Schedule and actually review: Assets and Debts, Insurance, Retirement and Estate Plan.
❑Make changes as necessary.
❑Attach up-to-date Lists of assets and debts, life insurance policies and retirement plans to your estate plan documents.
❑Inform your family of the location of your documents and make certain they can access the documents.
❑Inform your family about documents stored in your computer and how to access the documents.

Get Started.

"Knowledge is Power" but only if the knowledge prompts action. As in most important undertakings the first step is ALWAYS the most difficult. But once you get started everything will quickly fall into place. Your reward will be the peace of mind that comes from knowing that you have your affairs are in order and made things as easy as possible for your family.

About the Author

Julie Calligaro has been an estate planning and probate attorney for 30 years. Ms. Calligaro was named an Estate and Gift Taxation Lawyer of the year by "*dbusiness*," Detroit's premier business journal, in 2010. And has been a member of the Ethics Committee at Henry Ford Wyandotte Hospital

Made in the USA
Coppell, TX
10 November 2021